Gilbert Goes on a ...

by Michèle Dufresne

Pioneer Valley Educational Press, Inc.

"Let's have a picnic," Kenny said to his friend Amber.

"O.K." said Amber.
They put their lunch in a backpack and walked to the farm next door.

"Here's a good place," said Kenny. They put down a blanket and got their lunch out of the backpack.

"Look, here comes Gilbert," said Kenny. "Hello, Gilbert."

"Oink, oink," said Gilbert.

"Gilbert is hungry," said Amber.

"Here," Kenny said to Gilbert. "Have my sandwich."

"Oink, oink," said Gilbert.

"He likes the sandwich," said Amber.

"Oink, oink, **oink**!" said Gilbert.

"He's still hungry," said Amber.

"Here," Kenny said to Gilbert. "Have my apple."

"He likes the apple," said Amber.

"Oink, oink, **oink**!" said Gilbert.

"He's still hungry. Here, have **my** sandwich," Amber said to Gilbert.

"Oink, oink, **oink**!" said Gilbert.

"He's still hungry. Here, have **my** apple," Amber said to Gilbert.

"Uh, oh," said Kenny.
"I'm hungry and we gave all of our lunch to Gilbert!"